Guard Dog

Philip Wooderson

Illustrated by Dave Burroughs

A & C Black • London

CHAPTER ONE

I didn't want to go to the market, but Dad saw this as his chance to stop me from playing *Guard Dog* for the rest of Saturday morning.

You play that game so much, you're starting to look like a guard dog.

GUARD DOG

BLEEP BLEEP BLEEP

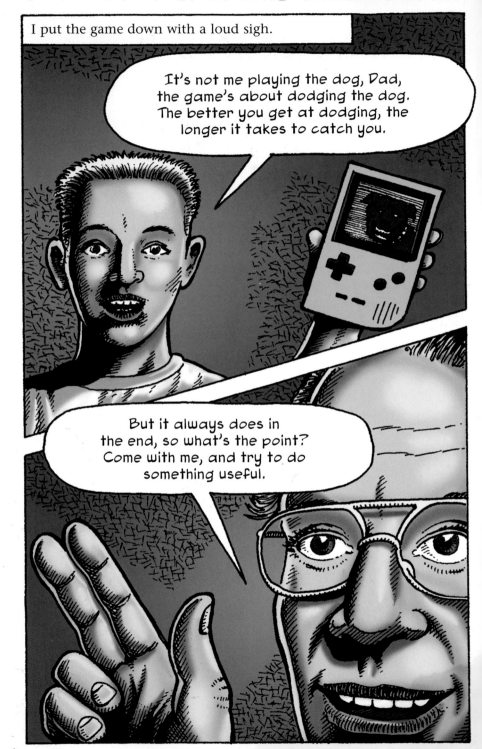

So I went with Dad to see about renting a stall for him to sell his woodwork. Dad got the last one. He was chuffed until the market man told him he had to pay rent up front.

What, all of it now?

If you don't like it, you don't have to have a stall, mate.

I could see Dad was getting ready to start an argument. I gave him a jab with my elbow.

Come on, Dad, just pay up.

Dad slapped down the money, and we left.

Outside, a man who had been in the queue ahead of us caught up with Dad.

Dad had been working hard every evening for weeks turning out lamp stands, salad bowls, spoons, and doorstops.

9

It took me more than an hour to load the car by myself. Then I thought I'd run off to see my friend Steve. But Dad was ready and waiting.

Make sure you're back by supper. Don't want to be late tonight. You've got an early start tomorrow.

Me?

Yes, you, young man. You can help me set up the stall.

CHAPTER TWO

Dad woke me up at half-past five the next morning.

We were out of the house before the sun came up. But our car wasn't there.

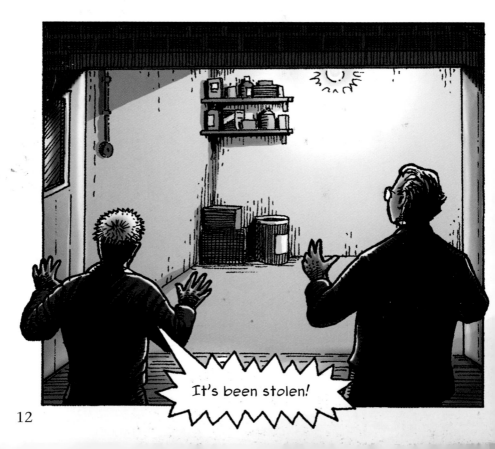

Dad quickly called the police.

My stock's been stolen! And I'll lose my first day of trading AND the rent on the stall.

Could we have the car's registration? Then we can put out a search, sir.

The rest of the morning went by slowly. Dad thumbed through the papers, and I bleeped away on my computer game, trying to dodge the guard dog. Top score 190.

That noise is driving me mad!

BLEEP
BLEEP
BLEEP

Can I call Steve and ask him to come over?

OBSERVER

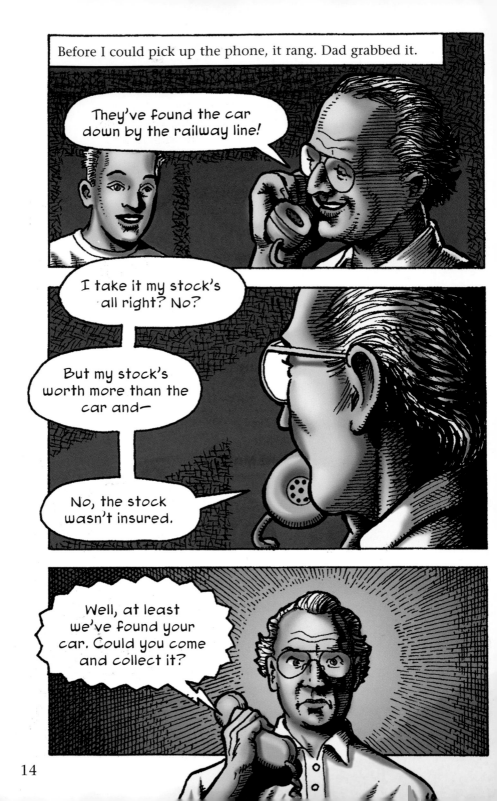

CHAPTER THREE

We found the car on a grimy street by the railway line.
The thief had smashed a window and hot-wired the ignition.
And there was already a parking ticket on the windscreen.

Then we cruised around town for an hour. Dad stopped
to search every skip, but we didn't find any of his stock.
Not even a single lamp stand!

As soon as we got home, Dad called the market office to tell them why we weren't there.

After the phone call, Dad left me in peace. He went off to the timber yard to buy himself some more wood. When he came home, he shut himself in the garden shed and got busy. He didn't ask me to help. After a couple of hours bleeping away at *Guard Dog* (best score 203), I was bored out of my brain.

In the place where our stall should have been was a big, gleaming mobile shop.

Steve picked up a video of *Death Dungeon 2.*

You're too young!

Better than being too old.

21

We browsed around the rest of the stalls. Most of them were boring, except for one selling old comics. As we were walking toward it, Steve tugged my arm.

Look, Ryan.

Wally and Den's Wooden Objects.

Ob-jets.

You sound just like your dad.

Thanks.

Wally saw us and called us over.

Your dad chickened out?

I would have told him about the car being taken and all the stock being stolen, but I noticed what Wally was wrapping...

Hey, Steve, I recognise that!

It looks like one of Dad's!

I looked back at Wally's stall. Somebody else was there now, a man in a black leather jacket. Wally handed him a fat brown envelope. As the man walked away, I saw the back of his jacket.

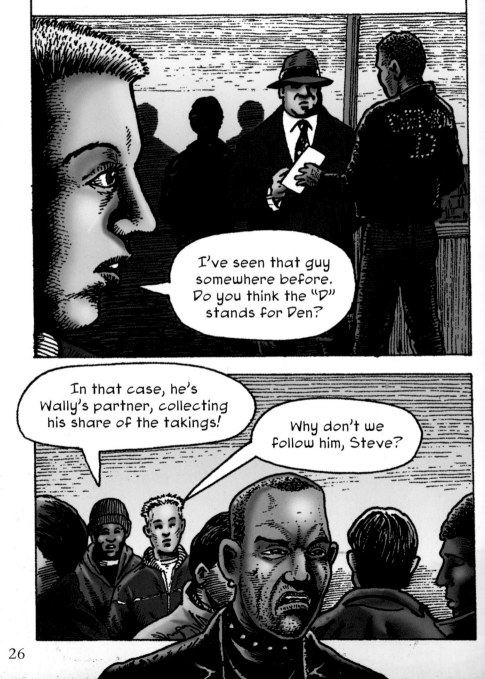

We followed, keeping our distance, so we were some way behind as he turned into the High Street. For a moment I thought we'd lost him. When I spotted him again, he was climbing into the passenger seat of a big black pick-up truck parked with two tyres on the kerb. It nosed out into the traffic. Steve and I swappped glances.

He looks really evil, Steve.

I bet he stole your dad's stock.

For Wally to sell?

Who else? I think we should call the police.

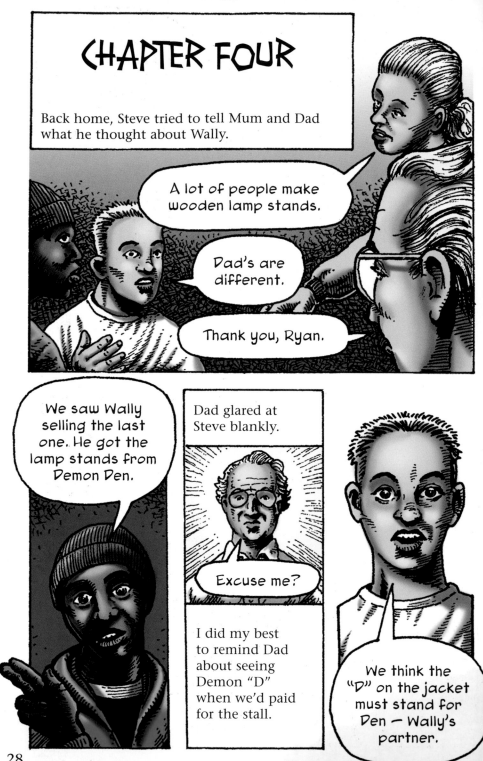

29

Three days later, Wally turned up at our house.
He told us he'd got our address from the market office.

Any more trouble from him and I'll get you banned from the market!

That did it. As soon as Wally left, Mum was yelling at me.

When you get together with Steve, you live in a fantasy world. You don't see ordinary people. You treat them like they're all monsters in your computer game. Dad's got to get along with the other traders.

After that, I decided to stay out of everyone's way.

When I got home from school the next day, Dad was busy carrying cardboard boxes out of his shed.

Shouldn't you wait till the morning? I mean, what if that thief comes back?

But Dad wasn't worried.

I've already loaded up the car. This lots going safely inside the house.

So what's in the car?

Empty boxes.

Clever.

What risk, Dad? Don't you trust me?

This isn't a game you know, Ryan.

Dad treated me like a child. I was feeling really down, so I went upstairs and played a quick game of *Guard Dog*. I beat my high score by 15, but what did that prove? Soon, Mum would be home, and she'd be yelling at me to finish my history project, which meant phoning Gran again.

BLEEP BLEEP BLEEP

Suddenly, I heard someone walking up the driveway. I went and looked out of the window, expecting to see Mum or Dad. Instead, I saw a dark figure peering into our car. The studs on his jacket gleamed under the streetlamp.

Demon Den!

I rushed downstairs.

35

CHAPTER FIVE

I should have gone and told Dad, but he was in the shed. There wasn't time to warn him. Instead I grabbed the camcorder, headed outside, and hoped that this risk was worth taking.

I couldn't just barge through the front door
– I didn't want Demon to see me – so I
hurried out through the back door and down
the alleyway. I came out on the street three
or four houses along. But Demon was already
walking away.

I followed him to the station, where he went into a phone
booth next to the taxi rank. I waited, wanting to film him,
but there was no light in the booth. Fortunately, I could hear
him all right, spitting words into the phone

He slammed the phone down and stormed out of the booth.

He walked right by without seeing me, back the way he had come.

I waited, wanting to let him get a few paces ahead. Before I could follow, the phone in the booth started ringing.

Demon kept on walking. I hesitated. After a few moments, I picked up the phone and said nothing.

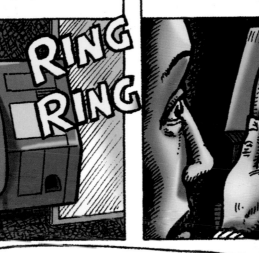

RING RING

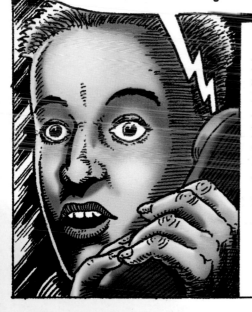

Demon? Is that you? I'm at The Stoker's Arms. Come round for a drink, talk about it. You and me should stay friends, OK?

I looked down the street again, but Demon had turned a corner. I put the phone down. I chased after him. But when I got to our road, I could see he had not gone that way. I'd lost him, so I went to tell Steve what had happened.

I didn't much like the idea, but as Steve climbed over the sill, the door of the pub swung open.

Quick!

I had no choice now. I scrambled into the back with Steve.

Just keep your head down.

As we ducked out of sight, someone climbed into the pick-up's cab and slammed the door.

Suddenly, the engine roared, and the pick-up lurched
forwards. As the tyres bumped off the curb, we got
shaken and rolled all over the cold metal floor.
Luckily, the journey was short.

The truck turned down a dark back street and came to a stop.
Once the man jumped out, I risked a look over the side.

Each arch was used as a worshop. There were signs
saying TYRES and BODY REPAIRS. But I still couldn't
see who the man was. He unlocked the garage door
and it slowly rattled open. Then the man drove the
truck inside, turned off the headlights, got out, and
walked off into the dark.

A door slammed at the back of the garage.

I'm sure that wasn't Wally.

He's gone to see someone else. Listen. Can't you hear them?

I heard someone shout: "Where's that darn dog?" Then a shrill squeaking noise as the steel door behind us started to roll slowly down. Steve jumped out of the truck.

SCREEE

Better get out while we can.

We haven't found out who they are yet.

I don't like it here.

Nor do I, but...

The door clanged onto the concrete floor.

There was no turning back. We crept along the side wall to a tall stack of cardboard boxes. Beyond was a door marked OFFICE with a toughened glasss window. Through this we could see two men sitting facing each other over a desk – the truck driver and a small man with a pencil moustache.

OFFICE

Well, neither of them is Wally.

I've seen them both somewhere before though.

So what?

This wasn't much help. Then I remembered the camcorder and brought it out of my pocket. I started to film them. Steve nudged me.

Do you hear that?

Dog's dangerous. You should ditch him.

I keep him for guarding this place.

But if someone breaks in, Ray...

He'd rip them to bits. That's their fault.

Steve and I glanced at each other.

Suppose the dog's loose in here now?

I think you've done enough filming.

But I kept recording for another minute.

It isn't my style. We're not thugs. It's important we keep our hands clean.

So, how do we ditch the dog?

The thin man stood up.

A quick phone call.

48

Come on, Ryan! We need to hide.

Steve pulled me back behind the cardboard boxes just as the office door opened. We managed to reach the truck and scramble up into the back before the men appeared.

They unlocked a small metal door built into the big garage door and stepped out into the street.

The door banged shut behind them, and the key turned again. Then silence. A minute later, a car started up outside. We listened to them drive away.

CHAPTER SEVEN

It was still early evening, too soon for Mum and Dad to worry where I might have gone, and Steve said his parents wouldn't be home until eight. By then, Demon Den might have turned up to steal our car again and even if Dad was waiting, he wouldn't have the camcorder to record the evidence. We needed to call for help.

OFFICE

Hoping to find something heavy, I opened the nearest box, but instead of a wooden lamp stand...

We ripped open more and more boxes. Every one was packed with identical video tapes still wrapped in polythene.

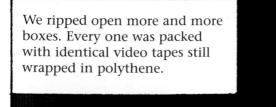

Hey, Ryan, look over there.

Steve pointd to a narrow space between the two stacks.

Where's that go?

The space had been left as a passage. Through the narrow opening there was a low archway, which led into a hidden room.

The room was dimly lit and filled with stacks of cardboard boxes. But down the far end was an alcove glowing with beady red lights. There were 20 video players, all whirring away. There was also a big TV and a video player on a stand.

The TV screen was blank, but the video seemed to be playing. Steve pressed the eject button.

I suddenly had an idea. Taking the tape from the camcorder, I plugged it into the player. I pressed rewind, then play, and switched on the TV.

I hesitated, thinking fast. Demon D must have stolen Dad's car to help the video pirates get Dad's place at the market. If Wally had sold Dad's lamp stands, he might have bought them from Demon without knowing where they had come from. If so, we must have got it wrong about the "D" standing for Den. Demon D was NOT Wally's partner. And Wally was not a crook.

Rummaging through my pockets, I brought out Wally's card.

I'm going to call Wally.

What for?

When Wally answered, I told him what we had discovered.

You mean Demon D set me up? He wants everyone to think I had your dad's car stolen to stop him from competing with me.

Demon's out to do it again, and he's taking his dog.

Ryan, hear that?

Steve was tugging my sleeve.

The phone slipped away from my ear. I heard it all right.

GGG-GG GGRRR

CHAPTER EIGHT

The phone was slapped out of my hand.

GGGG

GGRR

GRRR

Demon was growling, baring his teeth just like a—

They said, "Ditch the Dog. The Dog's dangerous."

Demon threw me back onto the ground.
They couldn't get by without me. They'd never have got your dad's space.

And now it's me that's caught you trespassing. Know what that means? What it means is I can use reasonable force because I'm defending myself, see? Go on!

Both of us raced through the doorway, but Demon was close behind. He lunged off to the right, blocking our only escape route, then swung round, showing his teeth.

Our only chance was to try to climb out of his reach.

Go over those boxes, Steve. Use the shelves as a ladder.

67

I followed. Demon was too quick though. He scrambled up over the boxes, snatching hold of my ankle, and started to pull me down.

Run!

I kicked him hard. He blinked and his grip briefly slipped, then closed again – round my trainer. I struggled, and…

YAAAHG!

He fell into the TV stand, knocking the
video player and somehow switching it on.
He stared at the screen in amazement.

Hitting the floor at a run, we were both through the arch, across the garage, and to the exit door. Then it occurred to me – the only way out would be locked.

Steve was fumbling with the catch. Demon lurched round the boxes at the back of the garage.

We ducked behind the pick-up, but there was nowhere to hide. I thought this was it – Demon would get us for sure. Then, he'd go and trash Dad's car, and maybe beat up Dad too. I'd really mucked everything up.

But weirdly, Demon ignored us. He walked straight to the door, pushed a key in the lock, and stumbled out into the street, leaving the door swinging open.

By the time we got outside, he had disappeared.

I bet he's gone to your house.

Steve and I ran all the way to the High Street and carried on up our road. But help was already at hand. A police van was outside our house!

This man was shining his torch into my car!

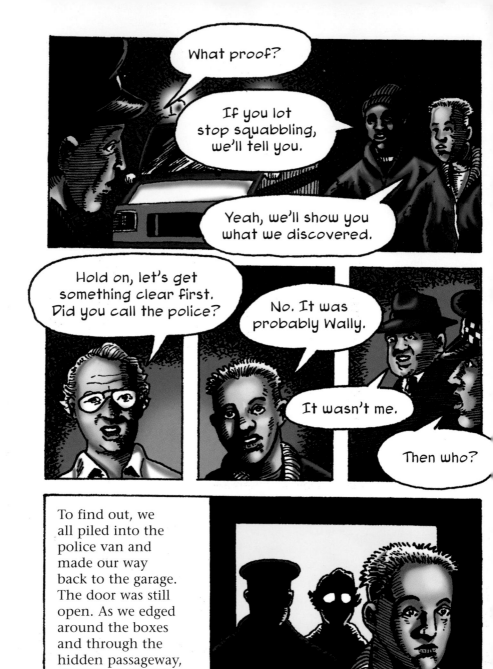

To find out, we all piled into the police van and made our way back to the garage. The door was still open. As we edged around the boxes and through the hidden passageway, the room seemed dangerously quiet.

The police were more concerned with all the video recorders and what was playing on the TV screen. I had left my video in there!

So, how do we ditch the dog?

A quick phone call.

Who to?

It's my duty to warn the police that there's a madman about to trash someone's car. Then they can catch him red-handed. He's bound to fight back – he'll get five years.

So that's where the tip-off came from.

CHAPTER NINE

We were all talking at once.

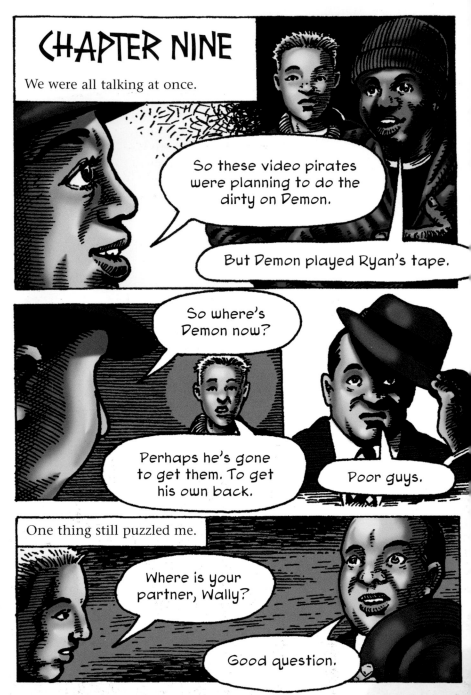

So these video pirates were planning to do the dirty on Demon.

But Demon played Ryan's tape.

So where's Demon now?

Perhaps he's gone to get them. To get his own back.

Poor guys.

One thing still puzzled me.

Where is your partner, Wally?

Good question.

Before Wally could say more, Dad apologised and asked him to come home for supper. So I had to wait to get the full story.

My partner, Den, was a great craftsman. He made wonderful stuff. He also took his time and wouldn't be pushed. But working six markets a week, you need a big supply. I had to buy from someone else.

That's why I bought Demon's stuff, which turned out to be your dad's lamp stands. When Den found out, he went crazy. We got into a huge argument.

79

Dad raised his hands with a shrug. He had to admit that our detective work had paid off.

But it seems I'm not the only clever one round here! Eh, Ryan?